AL PRACTICE TESTS
Based on
Next Generation Learning Standards

Published by
TOPICAL REVIEW BOOK COMPANY
P. O. Box 328
Onsted, MI 49265-0328
www.topicalrbc.com

EXAM	PAGE
Reference Sheet	i
Test 1	1
Test 2	11
Test 3	21
Test 4	31
Test 5	42
Test 6	52

Reference Sheet for Algebra I (NGLS)

Conversions

1 mile = 5280 feet
1 mile = 1760 yards
1 pound = 16 ounces
1 ton = 2000 pounds

Conversions Across Measurement Systems

1 inch = 2.54 centimeters
1 meter = 39.37 inches
1 mile = 1.609 kilometers
1 kilometer = 0.6214 mile
1 pound = 0.454 kilogram
1 kilogram = 2.2 pounds

Quadratic Equation	$y = ax^2 + bx + c$	Exponential Equation	$y = ab^x$
Quadratic Formula	$x = \dfrac{-b \pm \sqrt{b^2 - 4ac}}{2a}$	Annual Compound Interest	$A = P(1+r)^n$
Equation of the Axis of Symmetry	$x = -\dfrac{b}{2a}$	Arithmetic Sequence	$a_n = a_1 + d(n-1)$
Slope	$m = \dfrac{y_2 - y_1}{x_2 - x_1}$	Geometric Sequence	$a_n = a_1 r^{n-1}$
Linear Equation Slope Intercept	$y = mx + b$	Interquartile Range (IQR)	$IQR = Q_3 - Q_1$
Linear Equation Point Slope	$y - y_1 = m(x - x_1)$	Outlier	Lower Outlier Boundary = $Q_1 - 1.5(IQR)$
			Upper Outlier Boundary = $Q_3 + 1.5(IQR)$

ALGEBRA 1
Next Generation Learning Standards
Test 1
Part I

Answer all 24 questions in this part. Each correct answer will receive 2 credits. No partial credit will be allowed. For each question, write on the space provided the numeral preceding the word or expression that best completes the statement or answers the question.

1. What are the values of x in the equation $x(x - 6) = 4(x + 6)$?
(1) $\{-6, 6\}$ (2) $\{-12, 2\}$ (3) $\{-2, 12\}$ (4) $\{-6, 0, 6\}$ 1 _____

2. Which of ordered pairs is *not* a function?
(1) $\{(0, 9),(9, 0),(1, 2),(3, 4)\}$ (3) $\{(2, 3),(3, 4),(4, 5),(5, 6)\}$
(2) $\{(0, 1),(-1, 0),(1, 2),(3, 2)\}$ (4) $\{(2, 3),(2, 4),(4, 5),(4, 6)\}$ 2 _____

3. If $f(x) = |3x - 4| + 2$, find $f(-10)$.
(1) 28 (2) 34 (3) 36 (4) 38   3 _____

4. What is the value of the 1st quartile in the data set below?
Scores on a math quiz: 65, 90, 100, 72, 88, 55, 73
(1) 65 (2) 73 (3) 90 (4) 55   4 _____

5. What is the length of the missing side of the quadrilateral shown if the perimeter is $5x^2 + 2x + 1$?
(1) $4x^2 - 6x + 2$ (3) $-4x^2 + 8x + 4$
(2) $-4x^2 + 6x + 2$ (4) $4x^2 + 8x - 4$

Sides: $2x^2 + x - 1$, $3x^2 - 5x$, $4x^2$, ?   5 _____

6. What is the product of $(x + 1)$ and $(2x^2 + 3x - 1)$?
(1) $2x^2 + 5x^2 - x - 1$ (3) $2x^3 + 3x^2 + 3x + 1$
(2) $2x^3 + 5x^2 + 2x - 1$ (4) $2x^3 + 3x^2 - 3x - 1$ 6 _____

7. Which graph is a correct representation of the function $f(x) = 3^x$?

(1) (2) (3) (4)   7 _____

8. The formula for the volume of a cone is $V = \frac{1}{3}\pi r^2 h$. The radius, r, of the cone may be expressed as

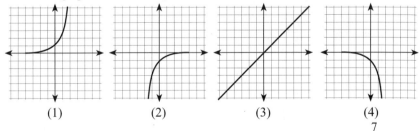

(1) $\sqrt{\dfrac{3V}{\pi h}}$ (2) $\sqrt{\dfrac{V}{3\pi h}}$ (3) $3\sqrt{\dfrac{V}{\pi h}}$ (4) $\dfrac{1}{3}\sqrt{\dfrac{V}{\pi h}}$ 8 _____

ALGEBRA 1 - NGLS
Test 1

9. How can $b^2 + 9b + 14$ be re-written?
(1) $(b + 7)(b - 7)$
(2) $(b - 7)(b - 2)$
(3) $(b + 7)(b - 2)$
(4) $(b + 7)(b + 2)$

9 _____

10. What is the sum of $3x\sqrt{5} + 2x\sqrt{5}$?
(1) $5x\sqrt{5}$
(2) $5x^2\sqrt{5}$
(3) $5x\sqrt{14}$
(4) $5x^2\sqrt{14}$

10 _____

11. Using the equation $y = ax^2 + bx + c$ to represent a parabola on a graph, which statement is true?
(1) If b is negative, the parabola opens downward.
(2) If a is negative, the parabola opens upward.
(3) If a is positive, the parabola opens upward.
(4) If c is negative, the parabola opens downward.

11 _____

12. If the function $h(x)$ represents the number of full hours that it takes a person to assemble x sets of tires in a factory, which would be an appropriate domain for the function?
(1) the set of real numbers
(2) the set of negative integers
(3) the set of integers
(4) the set of non-negative integers

12 _____

13. A café owner tracks the number of customers during business hours. The graph models the data. Based on the graph, the café owner saw a continual
(1) increase in customers from 6:00 to 11:00
(2) increase in customers from 12:00 to 3:00
(3) decrease in customers from 1:00 to 4:00
(4) decrease in customers from 11:00 to 2:00

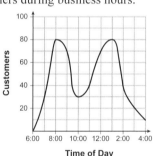

13 _____

14. Which equation is represented by the accompanying graph?
(1) $y = \begin{cases} -1; x < -2 \\ 2; x > -2 \end{cases}$
(2) $y = \begin{cases} -1; x \leq -2 \\ 2; x > -2 \end{cases}$
(3) $y = \begin{cases} -1; x < -2 \\ 2; x \geq -2 \end{cases}$
(4) $y = \begin{cases} -1; x \leq -2 \\ 2; x \geq -2 \end{cases}$

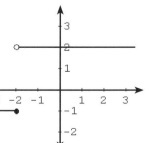

14 _____

15. Seven less than twice a number is greater than 5 more than the same number. Which integer satisfies this inequality?
(1) 1
(2) 2
(3) 12
(4) 13

15 _____

ALGEBRA 1 - NGLS
Test 1

16. A mouse population starts with 2,000 mice and grows at a rate of 5% per year. The number of mice after t years can be modeled by the equation, $P(t) = 2000(1.05)^t$. What is the average rate of change in the number of mice between the second year and the fifth year, rounded to the *nearest whole number*?
(1) 116   (2) 348   (3) 2205   (4) 2553   16 _____

17. What is the value of x in the equation $\frac{5(2x-4)}{3} + 9 = 14$?
(1) 1.9   (2) 3.5   (3) 5.3   (4) 8.9   17 _____

18. Which statement is true about the accompanying graph?
(1) It is decreasing when $-1 < x < 3$ and positive when $x > 1$.
(2) It is increasing when $x > 1$ and negative when $x < 0$.
(3) It is increasing when $x > 1$ and negative when $-1 < x < 3$.
(4) It is decreasing when $-1 < x < 3$ and positive when $x > 3$.

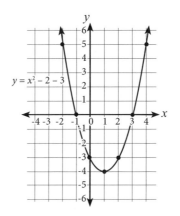

18 _____

19. The two-way table below represents the travel history of the seniors in the local Travel Club.

Travel Club History			
	Gender		Total
	Men	Women	
Aruba	14	19	33
Jamaica	17	18	35
Canada	32	22	54
Spain	4	11	15
Total	67	70	137

What is the percentage of the number of men and women that have traveled to Canada?
(1) 16%   (2) 23%   (3) 39%   (4) 42%   19 _____

20. What is the equation of the line with a slope of $-\frac{1}{2}$ that passes through the point $(6, -6)$?
(1) $y = -\frac{1}{2}x - 3$ (2) $y = \frac{1}{2}x - 3$ (3) $y = -\frac{1}{2}x + 3$ (4) $y = -2x - 3$ 20 _____

ALGEBRA 1 - NGLS
Test 1

21. Alex makes ceramic bowls to sell at a monthly craft fair in a nearby city. Every month, she spends $50 on materials for the bowls from a local art store. At the fair, she sells each completed bowl for a total of $25 including tax. Which equation expresses Alex's profit as a function of the number of bowls that she sells in one month?
(1) $p(x) = 50x + 25$
(2) $p(x) = 15x + 25$
(3) $p(x) = 25x$
(4) $p(x) = 25x - 50$ 21 _____

22. Which expression is equivalent to $x^4 - y^4$?
(1) $(x^2 - y^2)(x^2 + y^2)$
(2) $(x^2 - y^2)(x^2 - y^2)$
(3) $(2x^2)^2 - (2y^2)^2$
(4) $(x^2y^2) - (x^2y^2)$ 22 _____

23. A bottle rocket that was made in science class had a trajectory path that followed the quadratic equation $y = -x^2 + 4x + 6$. What is the vertex of the rocket's path?
(1) (1, 5)   (2) (2, 10)   (3) (-2, -10)   (4) (1, -5)   23 _____

24. What is the solution to this system of linear equations:
$$y - x = 4 \text{ and } y + 2x = 1?$$
(1) (-1, 3)   (2) (0, 4)   (3) (1, -1)   (4) (-3, 3)   24 _____

Part II
Answer all 6 questions in this part. Each correct answer will receive 2 credits. Clearly indicate the necessary steps, including appropriate formula substitutions, diagrams, graphs, charts, etc. For all questions in this part, a correct numerical answer with no work shown will receive only 1 credit. All answers should be written in the space provided. [16]

25. The function shown to the right represents the amount of money in a savings account in Lender's Bank.

Find the average rate of change of the domain for week 2 through week 5.

Week	Balance
1	$128
2	$142
3	$156
4	$170
5	$184

26. Graph $2x + y < 7$ and state one point in the solution set.

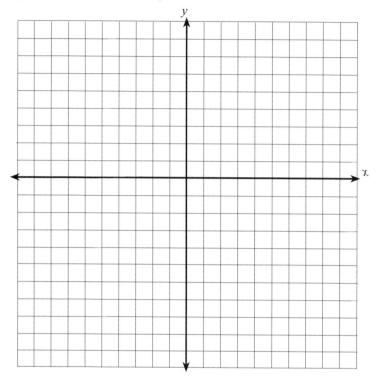

27. Solve for x: $2x^2 + 4x - 16 = 0$

ALGEBRA 1 - NGLS
Test 1

28. Solve for x: $\frac{1}{2}x + 12 > 0.4x + 10$

29. MaryJo decided to solve the equation $3x - 2 = -x - 6$ by entering each of the expressions into her graphing calculator. To solve the equation as a system, she entered $y_1 = 3x - 2$ and $y_2 = -x - 6$. When she used the calculator to find the intersection, she found $x = -1$ and $y = -5$. Show the work to check to see if MaryJo found the correct solution for x to the linear equation.

30. A company produces x units of a product per month, where $C(x)$ represents the total cost and $R(x)$ represents the total revenue for the month. The functions are modeled by $C(x) = 300x + 250$ and $R(x) = -0.5x^2 + 800x - 100$. The profit is the difference between revenue and cost where $P(x) = R(x) - C(x)$. What is the total profit, $P(x)$, for the month?

ALGEBRA 1 - NGLS
Test 1
Part III

Answer all 4 questions in this part. Each correct answer will receive 4 credits. Clearly indicate the necessary steps, including appropriate formula substitutions, diagrams, graphs, charts, etc. For all questions in this part, a correct numerical answer with no work shown will receive only 1 credit. All answers should be written in pen, except for graphs and drawings, which should be done in pencil. [16]

31. Find one point that lies in the solution set of the following system of inequalities:

$$y \geq x$$
$$y < -x - 2$$

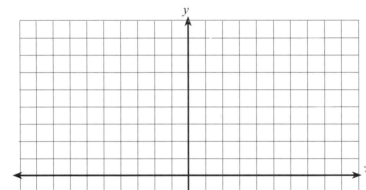

Justify your answer.

ALGEBRA 1 - NGLS
Test 1

32. Jonathan has been on a diet since January. So far, he has been losing weight at a steady rate. Based on monthly weigh-ins, his weight, w, in pounds can be modeled by the function $w = -3m + 205$ where m is the number of months after January.

How much did Jonathan weigh at the start of the diet?

How much weight has Jonathan been losing each month?

How many months did it take Jonathan to lose 45 pounds?

33. The final exam in an Algebra class of 15 students. The grades are:

65, 70, 78, 80, 83, 85, 85, 85, 85, 85, 87, 87, 87, 90, 90

Create a dot plot for the final test scores.

What is the value of the lower and upper quartile?

What is the Interquartile Range (IQR) of the data?

ALGEBRA 1 - NGLS
Test 1

34. Yolanda owns 4 rabbits. She expects the number of rabbits to double every year.

Write an equation and graph to model this situation.

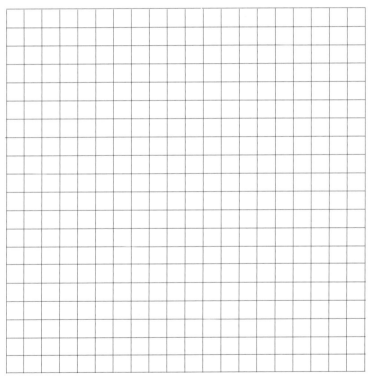

After how many years will she have 64 rabbits?

ALGEBRA 1 - NGLS
Test 1
Part IV

Answer one question in this part. The correct answer will receive 6 credits. Clearly indicate the necessary steps, including appropriate formula substitutions, diagrams, graphs, charts, etc. For all questions in this part, a correct numerical answer with no work shown will receive only 1 credit. All answers should be written in the spaces provided. [6]

35. Solve this system of equations graphically and check:
$$y = x + 4$$
$$y = -2x + 1$$

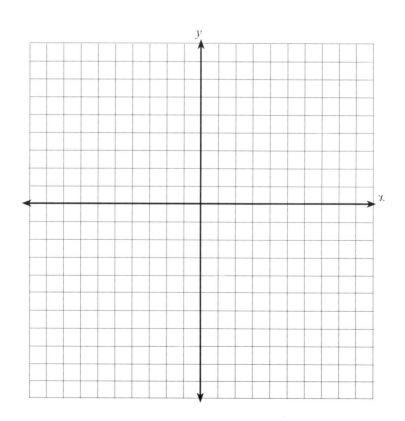

ALGEBRA 1
Next Generation Learning Standards
Test 2
Part I

Answer all 24 questions in this part. Each correct answer will receive 2 credits. No partial credit will be allowed. For each question, write on the space provided the numeral preceding the word or expression that best completes the statement or answers the question.

1. What is the sum of $4x\sqrt{5} + 3x\sqrt{5}$?
(1) $7x^2\sqrt{5}$ (2) $7x^2\sqrt{10}$ (3) $7x^2\sqrt{10}$ (4) $7x\sqrt{5}$ 1 _____

2. What is the difference when $2x^3 + x - 5$ is subtracted from $6x^3 - x^2 + 4x + 8$?
(1) $4x^3 - x^2 + 3x + 13$ (3) $8x^3 - x^2 + 5x + 3$
(2) $4x^3 - x^2 - 3x - 13$ (4) $8x^3 + 3x + 3$ 2 _____

3. Which system of equations would have the same solution as the system: $x + y = 5$
   $3x + 2y = 10$

(1) $3x + 2y = 5$ (3) $-3x - 3y = 5$
    $x + y = 10$ $3x + 2y = 10$
(2) $-3x - 3y = -15$ (4) $2x + 2y = 5$
    $3x + 2y = 10$ $3x + 2y = 10$ 3 _____

4. Which situation could be modeled with an exponential function?
(1) the amount of money in a savings account where $150 is deducted every month
(2) the amount of money in Suzy's piggy bank which she adds $10 to each week
(3) the amount of money in a certificate of deposit that gets 4% interest each year
(4) the amount of money in Jaclyn's wallet which increases and decreases by a different amount each week   4 _____

5. The graph of $y = f(x)$ is shown.

Which graph represents $y = f(x - 2) + 1$?

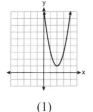   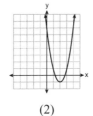   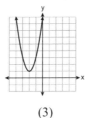   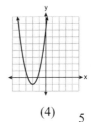

(1)   (2)   (3)   (4)   5 _____

6. In the dot plot below, what is the value of the median?

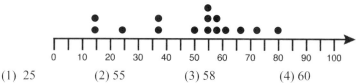

(1) 25 (2) 55 (3) 58 (4) 60   6 ____

7. Dale is trying to find the height of a triangular wall. The formula for the area of a triangle is $A = \frac{1}{2}bh$. He already knows the area and the base measurement of the wall. Which is the equation of the area of a triangle, written in terms of the *height*?

(1) $h = \frac{2A}{b}$ (2) $h = 2Ab$ (3) $h = \frac{b}{2A}$ (4) $h = \frac{1}{2}bA$ 7 ____

8. Which graph displays a square root function?

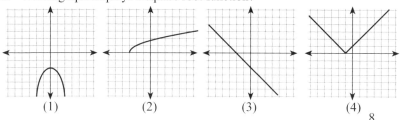

(1)   (2)   (3)   (4)   8 ____

9. If the function $f(x)$ represents the number of words that Janet can type in x minutes, what is the possible domain for the function?
(1) The set of integers   (3) The set of non-negative integers
(2) The set of real numbers   (4) The set of irrational numbers   9 ____

10. Which function models the relationship shown in the table?

x	$f(x)$
1	100
2	50
3	25
4	12.5
5	6.25

(1) $f(x) = \frac{100}{x}$ (3) $f(x) = 50(2)^x$

(2) $f(x) = 100\left(\frac{1}{2}\right)^x$ (4) $f(x) = 200\left(\frac{1}{2}\right)^x$ 10 ____

11. Which best describes a causal relationship?
(1) one variable takes place at the same time as another
(2) one variable is causing change in another
(3) one variable has a relationship with another
(4) one variable increases the possibility of another occurring   11 ____

12. Which is the equation of a line with a slope of –2 that passes through the point (–2, 0)?
(1) $y + 2x = -4$ (2) $y - 2x = 4$ (3) $y + 2 = -2x$ (4) $y - 4x = 2$ 12 ____

ALGEBRA 1 - NGLS
Test 2

13. The two-way table below represents the plans for seniors at Grant High School following graduation.

Post-Education Plans

	Gender		Total
	Boys	Girls	
2-year college	36	28	64
4-year college	52	67	119
military	12	5	17
career	29	13	42
undecided	7	16	23
Total	136	129	265

What is the percentage of the number of girls planning to attend a 4-year college?
(1) 11%   (2) 14%   (3) 20%   (4) 25%   13 _____

14. The length of a rectangular flat-screen television is six inches less than twice its width, x. If the area of the television screen is 1100 square inches, which equation can be used to determine the width, in inches?
(1) $x(2x - 6) = 1100$ (3) $2x + 2(2x - 6) = 1100$
(2) $x(6 - 2x) = 1100$ (4) $2x + 2(6 - 2x) = 1100$ 14 _____

15. Which rule describes the relationship between x and y in the accompanying table?
(1) $y = |-3x|$ (3) $y = |x| - 3$
(2) $y = |x - 3|$ (4) $y = |x| + 3$

x	y
0	-3
-1	-2
-2	-1
-3	0

15 _____

16. Which function described below is quadratic?
(1) $y = 2x$ (2) 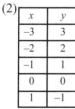   (3)

x	y
-3	8
-2	3
-1	0
0	-1
1	0

(4)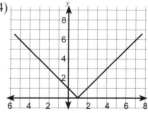

For (2):

x	y
-3	3
-2	2
-1	1
0	0
1	-1

16 _____

17. Which statement below is true about linear functions?
(1) Linear functions grow by equal factors over equal intervals.
(2) Linear functions grow by equal differences over equal intervals.
(3) Linear functions grow by equal differences over unequal intervals.
(4) Linear functions grow by unequal factors over equal intervals.   17 _____

ALGEBRA 1 - NGLS
Test 2

18. Labor at the car repair shop can be represented by the function:

Total charge for repairs $\begin{cases} 150, 0 < h \le 1 \\ 150 + 80(h-1), h > 1 \end{cases}$

If h represents the number of hours worked, what is the charge for a 3-hour car repair?
(1) $150 (2) $230 (3) $310 (4) $390   18 ____

19. If $g(x) = x^2 + 3x$, what is the value of $g(-3)$.
(1) 0 (2) 3 (3) 18 (4) 21   19 ____

20. The height of a ball above the ground in feet is defined by the function $h(t) = -16t^2 + 80t + 3$ where t is the number of seconds after the ball is thrown. What is the value of $h(t)$, two seconds after the ball is thrown?
(1) 80 feet (2) 99 feet (3) 103 feet (4) 200 feet   20 ____

21. Which function below will result in a downward vertical shift of the graph of the parent function: $y = x^2$?
(1) $y = \frac{1}{2}x^2$ (2) $y = 2x^2$ (3) $y = x^2 + 2$ (4) $y = x^2 - 1$ 21 ____

22. Which set of data of temperatures has the largest dispersion as measured by its interquartile range?
(1) 15, 17, 19, 21, 21, 22, 28 (3) 10, 19, 22, 23, 23, 29, 44
(2) 21, 23, 36, 37, 44, 48, 50 (4) 42, 47, 49, 50, 52, 59, 60   22 ____

23. A box plot is shown below.

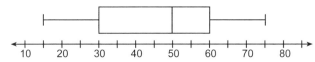

Which number represents the third quartile?
(1) 30 (2) 50 (3) 60 (4) 75   23 ____

24. Which point is in the solution set to the system of inequalities: $y > 2x - 1$ and $y \le \frac{1}{2}x + 5$?

(1) (−3, 10) (2) (8, 2) (3) (−2, 1) (4) (4, 1)   24 ____

ALGEBRA 1 - NGLS
Test 2
Part II

Answer all 6 questions in this part. Each correct answer will receive 2 credits. Clearly indicate the necessary steps, including appropriate formula substitutions, diagrams, graphs, charts, etc. For all questions in this part, a correct numerical answer with no work shown will receive only 1 credit. All answers should be written in pen, except for graphs and drawings, which should be done in pencil. [16]

25. The formula $d = t\left(\dfrac{v_i + v_f}{2}\right)$ is used to calculate the distance, d, covered by an object in a given period of time, t.

Solve the formula for v_f, the final velocity, in terms of d, t, and v_i, the initial velocity.

26. Sales in the printing business have doubled for James in each of the last three months. During the last month, he made a profit of $520. If the pattern continues, what will be his *three-month total* profit at the end of the next three months?

ALGEBRA 1 - NGLS
Test 2

27. Breanna creates the pattern of blocks below in her art class.

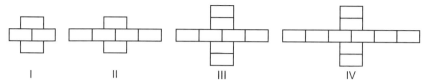

I II III IV

A friend tells her that the number of blocks in the pattern is increasing exponentially. Is her friend correct?

Explain your reasoning.

28. Find the area of the rectangle with a length of $(x^2 - 2)$ and a width of $(2x^2 - x + 2)$. Write your answer in standard form.

29. Given $h(x) = -2x^2 - x + 2$, find $h(-2)$.

ALGEBRA 1 - NGLS
Test 2

30. Rows of chairs are set out for a wedding. There are 6 chairs in the first row, 14 chairs in the second row, and 22 chairs in the third row. The rows continue in the same patterns for a total of 7 rows. How many chairs are set out for the wedding guests?

Part III

Answer all 4 questions in this part. The correct answer will receive 4 credits. Clearly indicate the necessary steps, including appropriate formula substitutions, diagrams, graphs, charts, etc. For all questions in this part, a correct numerical answer with no work shown will receive only 1 credit. All answers should be written in pen, except for graphs and drawings, which should be done in pencil. [16]

31. Jennifer and Kim enjoy making bracelets. At the beginning of this year Jennifer had already made twenty-five bracelets. She continues to make eight bracelets every month. Kim just started making bracelets recently, so she had only made eleven at the beginning of the year. Kim is able to work faster, so she makes ten bracelets every month.

Write the equations for the production of bracelets(b) for both Jennifer and Kim.

During what month(s) this year will Kim have made more bracelets than Jennifer?

32. Create a scatter plot to demonstrate the relationship between the snow storms this year and the average amount of salt used on the roads in town.

Sketch a line or curve of best fit.

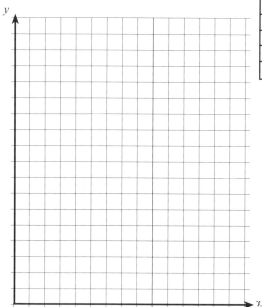

Snow storm	Salt (pounds)
1	3
2	4
3	8
4	10
5	15

Determine a function to define it, based on the line of best fit.

33. Solve the following systems of equations algebraically for all values of x and y:
$$y = x^2 + 5x - 17$$
$$x - y = 5$$

34. The data chart to the right represents the local Baseball Team shoe order.

Write the linear regression equation for the line of best fit for the data in the chart. *Round the numbers to the nearest hundredth.*

Baseball Team Shoe Order

Height in Inches	Shoe Size
68	11
60	8
64	10
78	13
74	12.5
78	14
74	11
60	7
70	10
64	9
72	11
74	13
72	12
78	13.5

State the correlation coefficient to the *nearest hundredth.*

Describe the strength of the correlation.

ALGEBRA 1 - NGLS
Test 2
Part IV

Answer one question in this part. The correct answer will receive 6 credits. Clearly indicate the necessary steps, including appropriate formula substitutions, diagrams, graphs, charts, etc. For all questions in this part, a correct numerical answer with no work shown will receive only 1 credit. All answers should be written in pen, except for graphs and drawings, which should be done in pencil. [6]

35. Jonathan makes a weekly allowance of $25. He also makes $9.50 an hour at his job. Because of his age, Jonathan can work no more than 20 hours a week.

Write a function for the amount of money he makes each week based on his allowance and the amount of hours, h, he works.

What is the domain of the function for this situation?

Use the grid below to graph the function over the domain you chose.

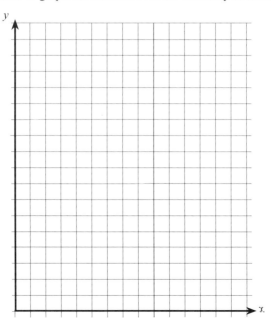

ALGEBRA 1
Next Generation Learning Standards
Test 3
Part I

Answer all 24 questions in this part. Each correct answer will receive 2 credits. No partial credit will be allowed. For each question, write on the space provided the numeral preceding the word or expression that best completes the statement or answers the question.

1. Which expression is equivalent to $(x^2 + 3x - 4)(x - 5)$?
(1) $x^3 + 8x^2 - 19x + 20$
(2) $x^3 - 2x^2 - 19x + 20$
(3) $x^3 - 2x^2 - 11x + 20$
(4) $x^3 - 8x^2 - 11x + 20$ 1 _____

2. What are the zeros of $(x - 2)(x^2 - 9)$?
(1) $\{-3, 2, 3\}$ (2) $\{-3, 3\}$ (3) $\{-3, 0, -3\}$ (4) $\{0, 3\}$ 2 _____

3. The formula for converting degrees Celsius to Fahrenheit is $F = \frac{9}{5}C + 32$. Which expression is correctly written to convert Fahrenheit temperatures into degrees Celsius?
(1) $C = \frac{9}{5}F + 32$
(2) $C = \frac{5}{9}F - 160$
(3) $C = \frac{5F - 160}{9}$
(4) $C = 32F + 160$ 3 _____

4. What are the restrictions of the domain of the function $F(x) = \frac{1}{x^2 - 9}$?
(1) $x \neq 3$ (2) $x \neq \pm 3$ (3) $x \neq 9$ (4) $x \neq 0$ 4 _____

5. What is the value of $f(2)$ when $f(x) = \begin{cases} 3x^2 + x - 1, x \geq 1 \\ 2x, x < 1 \end{cases}$?
(1) 4 (2) 7 (3) 11 (4) 13   5 _____

6. What are the possible values for x in the equation $4x^2 = 64$?
(1) $x = 0$ (2) $x = 4$ (3) $x = 4, -4$ (4) $x = 0, 4, -4$ 6 _____

7. Samuel's Car Service will charge a flat travel fee of $4.75 for anyone making a trip. They charge an additional set rate of $1.50 per mile that is traveled. What is an equation that represents the charges?
(1) $y = 1.5x + 1.5$
(2) $y = 4.75x + 4.75$
(3) $y = 1.5x + 4.75$
(4) $y = 4.75x + 1.5$ 7 _____

8. The accompanying frequency table indicates the grades on the math midterm in Ms. Dennis' class. The median of the data lies in which interval?
(1) 91-95   (3) 81-85
(2) 76-80   (4) 86-90

Frequency Table		
Interval	Tally	Frequency
96-100	JHT	5
91-95	I	1
86-90	JHT IIII	9
81-85	IIII	4
76-80	II	2
71-75	IIII	4

8 _____

ALGEBRA 1 - NGLS
Test 3

9. What is the interquartile range of the data set below?
Growth in feet of oak trees: 68, 80, 73, 90, 120, 94, 76, 112, 101, 94, 72
(1) 22 (2) 28 (3) 52 (4) 73   9 _____

10. A rocket is launched from the ground. The function $h(t) = -4.9t^2 + 180t$ models the height of a rocket launched from the ground t seconds after it is launched. If all other factors remain the same, which of the following function models the height of a rocket above the ground after t seconds if it is launched from a platform 100 feet in the air?
(1) $h(t) = -4.9t^2 + 280t$
(2) $h(t) = -4.9t^2 + 180t - 100$
(3) $h(t) = -4.9t^2 + 180t + 100$
(4) $h(t) = -4.9t^2 + 180(t + 100)$ 10 _____

11. What is the sum of $-2x^2 - 5x + 3$ and $-4x^2 + 4x - 6$?
(1) $6x^2 - x - 3$
(2) $-6x^2 - x - 3$
(3) $2x^2 + 9x - 3$
(4) $-6x^2 + 9x - 3$ 11 _____

12. Which situation describes a correlation that is *not* a causal relationship?
(1) Car color and number of car accidents
(2) Hours spent studying and test score
(3) Amount of exercise each week and the time it takes to run a mile
(4) Distance to reach a destination and the amount of gasoline used   12 _____

13. Which function has the largest maximum?
(1) $y = -x^2 + 2x - 1$
(2)

x	y
-3	-2
-2	1
-1	2
0	1
1	-2

(3) $y = -2x^2 - 3x + 4$
(4)

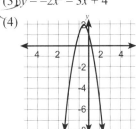

13 _____

14. The accompanying table shows the average yearly balance in a savings account where interest is compounded annually. No money is deposited or withdrawn after the initial amount is deposited. Which type of function best models the given data?

Year	Balance, in Dollars
0	380.00
10	562.49
20	832.63
30	1232.49
40	1824.39
50	2700.54

(1) linear function with a negative rate of change
(2) linear function with a positive rate of change
(3) exponential decay function
(4) exponential growth function   14 _____

ALGEBRA 1 - NGLS
Test 3

15. What is the degree of the polynomial $2x + x^3 + 5x^2$?
(1) 1 (2) 2 (3) 3 (4) 4   15 ____

16. Maxwell and Jessica went to the candy store. Maxwell bought one chocolate covered cookie and two lollipops for $2.50. Jessica bought one chocolate covered cookie and four lollipops for $3.00. How much does one lollipop cost?
(1) $0.25 (2) $0.40 (3) $.50 (4) $1.00   16 ____

17. If $x = \dfrac{a^2}{b}$, which situation would always double the value of x?
(1) Doubling the value of a.   (3) Doubling the value of b.
(2) Halving the value of a.   (4) Halving the value of b.   17 ____

18. Jessica is planning to build a square playing field. She wants to see how long the sides of the field will need to be for different areas. Her results are summarized in the following table.

What is the average rate of change in the side length as the area increases from 200 square feet to 700 square feet?

Area (square feet)	Side Length (feet)
100	10
200	14.14
300	17.32
400	20
500	22.36
600	24.49
700	26.46
800	28.28
900	30

(1) .025 (2) 20 (3) 40 (4) 800   18 ____

19. The selling prices for a group of cars were recorded when the cars were new and for an additional five years. The results are summarized in the tables below. Based as a percent, which car's price dropped at a constant rate each year?

(1)
Year	Cost
0	25,000
1	20,000
2	15,000
3	10,000
4	5,000
5	0

(2)
Year	Cost
0	25,000
1	30,000
2	35,000
3	40,000
4	45,000
5	50,0000

(3)
Year	Cost
0	25,000
1	20,000
2	16,000
3	12,800
4	10,240
5	8192

(4)
Year	Cost
0	25,000
1	30,000
2	36,000
3	43,000
4	52,840
5	62,208

19 ____

ALGEBRA 1 - NGLS
Test 3

20. Officials in a town use a function, C, to analyze traffic patterns. C(n) represents the rate of traffic through an intersection where n is the number of observed vehicles in a specified time interval. What would be the most appropriate domain for the function?

(1) $\{...-2, -1, 0, 1, 2, 3, ...\}$ (3)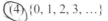

(2) $\{-2, -1, 0, 1, 2, 3\}$ (4) $\{0, 1, 2, 3, ...\}$ 20 _____

21. The graph represents a jogger's speed during her 20-minute jog around her neighborhood.

Which statement best describes what the jogger was doing during the 9 – 12 minute interval of her jog?

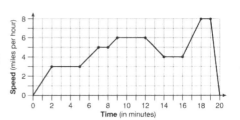

(1) She was standing still.
(2) She was increasing her speed.
(3) She was decreasing her speed.
(4) She was jogging at a constant rate.   21 _____

22. In the expression $5x^3 - 4x^2 + 2x + 3$, what is the coefficient of the quadratic term?

(1) –5   (2)   (3) 3   (4) 4   22 _____

23. The table below displays data collected from the census. What is the correlation coefficient between years of education past 8th grade and average yearly salary in the United States to the *nearest hundredth*?

Years of education past 8th grade	Average Yearly Salary
2 years (10th grade)	23,088
4 years (High School Graduate)	32,552
6 years (Associates' Degree)	39,884
8 years (Bachelor's Degree)	53,976
9 years (Master's Degree)	66,144
11 years (Doctorate)	80,600

(1) .96   (2) .97   (3) .98   (4) .99   23 _____

24. Which function below correctly illustrates the absolute value function?

(1) $|a| = \begin{cases} a, \text{ if } a \leq 0 \\ -a, \text{ if } a > 0 \end{cases}$ (3) $|a| = \begin{cases} \sqrt{a}, \text{ if } a \geq 0 \\ -a, \text{ if } a < 0 \end{cases}$

(2) $|a| = \begin{cases} a, \text{ if } a \geq 0 \\ -a, \text{ if } a < 0 \end{cases}$ (4) $|a| = \begin{cases} a, \text{ if } a \geq 0 \\ -\sqrt{a}, \text{ if } a < 0 \end{cases}$ 24 _____

ALGEBRA 1 - NGLS
Test 3

Part II

Answer all 6 questions in this part. Each correct answer will receive 2 credits. Clearly indicate the necessary steps, including appropriate formula substitutions, diagrams, graphs, charts, etc. For all questions in this part, a correct numerical answer with no work shown will receive only 1 credit. All answers should be written in the space provided. [16]

25. Solve $x^2 - 9x = 36$ algebraically for all values of x.

26. Solve: $\dfrac{3}{6x} + \dfrac{1}{2} = \dfrac{8}{x} + \dfrac{4}{3}$

27. Find the y-intercept(s), for the equation: $y = x^2 - 16$

28. Tim makes wooden salad bowls to sell at a monthly craft fair near his home town. Each month he spends $45 on specialty wood and other materials from his local lumber store. At the craft fair, Tim sells each completed salad bowl set for a total of $22, including tax. Express Tim's profit as a function of the number of salad bowl sets that he sells.

29. Factor $18x^2 - 2$ completely.

30. Solve for x and justify the steps necessary for solving the following equation.
$$x^2 - 8x - 20 = 0$$

ALGEBRA 1 - NGLS
Test 3
Part III

Answer all 4 questions in this part. Each correct answer will receive 4 credits. Clearly indicate the necessary steps, including appropriate formula substitutions, diagrams, graphs, charts, etc. For all questions in this part, a correct numerical answer with no work shown will receive only 1 credit. All answers should be written in pen, except for graphs and drawings, which should be done in pencil. [16]

31. A teacher surveyed a small senior class to find out how many hours they worked last week and their wages. The information from each student is summarized in the table.

Find the linear regression equation for the data in the table. Round all coefficients to the *nearest hundredth*.

Hours	Wages
20	250
15	180
14	200
32	350
0	0
5	100
40	380
12	100

Using your regression equation, how much money would someone make if he or she worked 25 hours last week? Round to the *nearest cent*.

32. Graph the function: $y = |x| + 3$, for domain $-4 \leq x \leq 3$

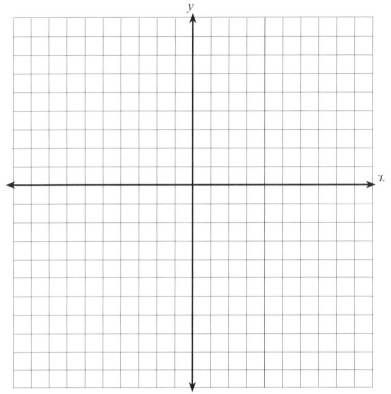

33. The following data is the set of quiz scores from Ms. Jones' algebra class:
56, 82, 78, 90, 99, 73, 85, 95, 76, 88, 100

Create a box plot for the data.

Find the interquartile range for the class.

Is the quiz score 56 considered to be an outlier? Justify your answer.

34. The cost of operating Jelly's Doughnuts is $1,600 per week plus $0.10 to make each doughnut.

Write a function, $C(d)$, to model the company's weekly costs for producing d doughnuts.

What is the total weekly cost if the company produces 4,000 doughnuts?

Jelly's Doughnuts makes a gross profit of $0.60 for each doughnut they sell. If they sold all 4,000 doughnuts they made, would they make money or lose money for the week? How much money would Jelly Doughnuts make or lose?

ALGEBRA 1 - NGLS
Test 3
Part IV

Answer one question in this part. The correct answer will receive 6 credits. Clearly indicate the necessary steps, including appropriate formula substitutions, diagrams, graphs, charts, etc. For all questions in this part, a correct numerical answer with no work shown will receive only 1 credit. All answers should be written in the spaces provided. [12]

35. Sketch the graph of all of the solutions to the equation $y = \frac{1}{4}(2)^x$ where $0 \leq x \leq 5$.

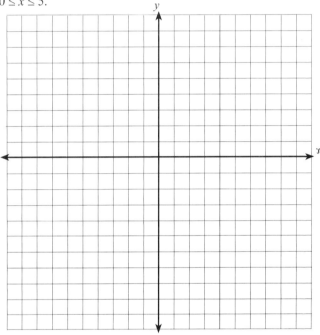

Find the average rate of change over the interval [2, 5].

ALGEBRA 1
Next Generation Learning Standards
Test 4
Part I

Answer all 24 questions in this part. Each correct answer will receive 2 credits. No partial credit will be allowed. For each question, write on the space provided the numeral preceding the word or expression that best completes the statement or answers the question.

1. In the expression $5x^3 - 4x^2 + 2x + 3$, what is the coefficient of the cubic term?
   (1) -4 (2) 2 (3) -3 (4) 5   1 ____

2. The graph of the equation $y = 3^x$ contains which point?
   (1) $(1, 9)$ (2) $(-2, \frac{1}{9})$ (3) $(2, 6)$ (4) $(-3, -\frac{1}{9})$ 2 ____

3. What is an equation of the line that passes through the points $(2, 7)$ and $(-1, 3)$?
   (1) $y - 2 = \frac{3}{4}(x - 7)$ (3) $y - 7 = \frac{3}{4}(x - 2)$
   (2) $y - 2 = \frac{4}{3}(x - 7)$ (4) $y - 7 = \frac{4}{3}(x - 2)$ 3 ____

4. Write the sum in standard form: $(3x^3 - 2x^2 - x + 2) + (4x^2 + 3x - 6)$
   (1) $3x^3 - 2x^2 + 4x - 8$ (3) $3x^3 + 2x^2 + 2x - 4$
   (2) $x^3 - 2x^2 + 4x - 8$ (4) $x^3 + 2x^2 + 4x - 4$ 4 ____

5. What are the zeros of the polynomial $x^3 - 9x = 0$?
   (1) 9 (2) 0, 9 (3) 3, -3 (4) 0, 3, -3 5 ____

6. Find the average rate of change over the interval -4 and -1 in the function $f(x) = x^2 + 2x - 8$.
   (1) -9 (2) -3 (3) 3 (4) 9   6 ____

7. As the value of x increases, which of the following functions would eventually exceed the other three?
   (1) $f(x) = 1000x$ (2) $f(x) = 100x^2$ (3) $f(x) = 50x^3$ (4) $f(x) = 2^x$ 7 ____

8. Solve for x in the following equation: $ax + 5x - 4 = 10$.
   (1) $x = \frac{9}{a}$ (2) $x = \frac{6}{5}$ (3) $x = \frac{14}{a+5}$ (4) $x = \frac{14}{5a}$ 8 ____

9. Ashley only has 7 quarters and some dimes in her purse. She needs at least $3.00 to pay for lunch. Which inequality could be used to determine the number of dimes, d, she needs in her purse to be able to pay for lunch?
   (1) $1.75 + d \geq 3.00$ (3) $1.75 + d \leq 3.00$
   (2) $1.75 + 0.10d \geq 3.00$ (4) $1.75 + 0.10d \leq 3.00$ 9 ____

ALGEBRA 1 - NGLS
Test 4

10. Joseph's taxi charges $10.00 for the initial service of any drive. Then, the fee for each mile is $0.75. Which type of function is represented by this situation?
    (1) linear   (2) exponential   (3) quadratic   (4) absolute value   10 ____

11. Look at the cumulative frequency table indicating the grades from a pre-assessment on graphing in Mr. Lawrence's class. How many students failed the pre-assessment if a passing score was 65%?

Cumulative Frequency Table

Interval	Frequency	Cumulative Frequency
75-79	5	30
70-74	6	25
65-69	3	19
60-64	10	16
55-59	1	6
50-54	5	5

(1) 11   (2) 16   (3) 22   (4) 27   11 ____

12. What is the domain for the function $\sqrt{x+2} - 2x$?
    (1) $[0, -2)$ (2) $(0, \infty)$ (3) $[-2, \infty)$ (4) $[2, \infty)$ 12 ____

13. Which point lies on the graph of the boundary line of the inequality $3y + 4x < 12$?
    (1) $(-3, 0)$ (2) $(8, 2)$ (3) $(0, 3)$ (4) $(3, 0)$ 13 ____

14. Mrs. Jones is describing a function to her students. She says the output is equal to seven less than twice the input. Which of the following equations models this relationship?
    (1) $f(x) = 7 - 2x$ (3) $f(x) = 2(7 - x)$
    (2) $f(x) = 2x - 7$ (4) $f(x) = 2(x - 7)$ 14 ____

15. Jerome throws a ball from a platform 80 feet above the ground. The flight of the ball can be modeled by the equation, $s(t) = -16t^2 + 64t + 80$ where t is the number of seconds after the Jerome throws the ball and s is the height of the ball above the ground. After how many seconds will the ball strike the ground?
    (1) 4   (2) 5   (3) 6   (4) 7   15 ____

16. Which relation is a function?
    (1) {(0, -2), (4, 10), (-1, -5), (2,4)}   (3) {(4, 8), (2, -3), (1, 1), (2, -1)}
    (2) {(2, 3), (2, 5), (2, 7), (2, 9)}   (4) {(0, 0), (0, 3), (3, 0), (4, -1)}   16 ____

17. What is the solution to $-3(x - 6) > 2x - 2$?
    (1) $x > 4$ (2) $x < 4$ (3) $x > -16$ (4) $x < -16$ 17 ____

ALGEBRA 1 - NGLS
Test 4

18. The function represented to the right shows the daily temperature change in a given month.

Day	Temperature
1	16°C
4	22°C
7	28°C
10	34°C
13	40°C

What is the average rate of change of the domain for day 4 through day 10?
(1) 2°C (3) 6°C
(2) $\frac{1}{2}$°C (4) 3°C

18 ____

19. Joey's math class is studying the basic quadratic function, $f(x) = x^2$. Each student is supposed to make two new functions by adding or subtracting a constant to the function. Joey chooses the functions $g(x) = x^2 - 5$ and $h(x) = x^2 + 2$. What transformations would map $f(x)$ to $g(x)$ and $f(x)$ to $h(x)$?
(1) shift left 5, shift right 2 (3) shift up 5, shift down 2
(2) shift right 5, shift left 2 (4) shift down 5, shift up 2

19 ____

20. Based on the box plots below, which quiz had the most spread as measured by the interquartile range?

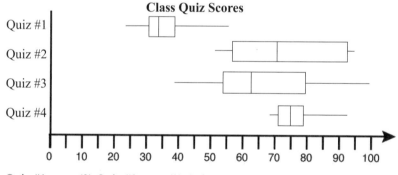

(1) Quiz #1 (2) Quiz #2 (3) Quiz #3 (4) Quiz #4

20 ____

21. Which function has the largest y-intercept?

(1)
x	$f(x)$
-1	-32
0	-30
1	-24
2	-14
3	0

(2) $f(x) = 2x^2 + 12$

(3)
x	$f(x)$
-2	12
-1	-3
0	-8
1	-3
2	12

(4)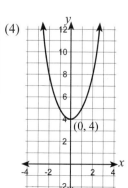

21 ____

ALGEBRA 1 - NGLS
Test 4

22. Which two variables have the strongest causal relationship?
(1) Height and income
(2) Air temperature and number of cars on the road
(3) Speed and time it takes to reach one's destination
(4) Hours spent watching television and size of one's home   22 ____

23. What is the value of the range in the data set below?
   Test scores: 68, 72, 90, 93, 75, 78, 91, 67
(1) 8   (2) 12   (3) 26   (4) 67   23 ____

24. Given the polynomial function $y = x^2 + 8x + 15$, what are the zeros of the polynomial?
(1) $x = -3, x = -5$ (3) $x = 3, x = -5$
(2) $x = -3, x = 5$ (4) $x = 3, x = 5$ 24 ____

Part II

Answer all 6 questions in this part. Each correct answer will receive 2 credits. Clearly indicate the necessary steps, including appropriate formula substitutions, diagrams, graphs, charts, etc. For all questions in this part, a correct numerical answer with no work shown will receive only 1 credit. All answers should be written in the space provided. [16]

25. What is the trinomial that represents the area of a rectangular box whose sides are $x - 5$ and $2x + 8$?

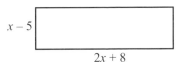

26. Determine and state whether the sequence 1, 3, 9, 27, . . . displays exponential behavior. Explain how you arrived at your decision.

ALGEBRA 1 - NGLS
Test 4

27. Solve this equation for n in terms of m: $3n + 2m = 4$

28. Given the function $g(x) = x^2 + 6x + 4$. Find the minimum value of the $g(x)$.

29. Jeff bought a new car $10,450. He knows this car's value will decrease by 20% each year. Jeff writes the following function to model the cost of his car after t years: $C(t) = 10,450(.80)^t$. If Jeff plans to sell the car after five years, what will be the value of the car at that time, to *the nearest dollar?*

30. Solve the following quadratic equation: $3x^2 + 3x - 6 = 0$

Part III

Answer all 4 questions in this part. Each correct answer will receive 4 credits. Clearly indicate the necessary steps, including appropriate formula substitutions, diagrams, graphs, charts, etc. For all questions in this part, a correct numerical answer with no work shown will receive only 1 credit. All answers should be written in pen, except for graphs and drawings, which should be done in pencil. [16]

31. Robin is deciding between two data plans. Phones Unlimited offers a plan for $20 per month for the first 500 megabytes of data and $2 per month for each additional 500 megabytes. Cells United offers a plan that costs $10 per gigabyte (1000 megabytes).

Write a function to model each of the data plans. Define the variable(s) in each function.

How much data would Robin have to use to make the Phones Unlimited data plan cheaper than the Cells United data plan?

ALGEBRA 1 - NGLS
Test 4

32. Create a dot plot for the set of data below.

   Times (in minutes) on the mile run:
   5.5, 5.0, 6.5, 8.0, 9.0, 7.5, 6.0, 6.5, 8.0, 9.0, 6.0, 6.5, 6.0

What is the mean of the run times listed above? Round your answer to the *nearest tenth*?

What is the interquartile range?

ALGEBRA 1 - NGLS
Test 4

33. Send With Us is a company that ships large packages overnight to cities all over the country. Overnight delivery is guaranteed. They charge for delivery depending on the weight of the package according to the following price list:

$30 per pound for packages weighing up to and including 10 pounds.

$25 per pound for packages weighing more than ten pounds and up to and including 20 pounds.

$20 per pound for packages weighing more than twenty pounds and up to and including 30 pounds.

$15 per pound for packages weighing more than thirty pounds.

Graph the function that describes the costs of all possible shipping charges.

If the package totals 15 pounds and there is an 8% tax on the shipping charges, what will be the total cost to ship the package?

34. Jean recorded temperatures over a 24-hour period one day in August in Syracuse, NY. Her results are shown in the table below.

Time (hour)	0	3	6	9	12	15	18	21	24
Temperature (°F)	80	75	70	78	92	89	85	80	74

Her data are modeled on the graph below.

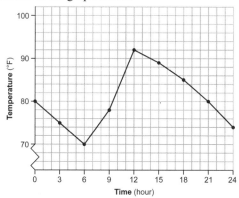

State the entire interval over which the temperature is increasing.

State the three-hour interval that has the greatest rate of change in temperature.

State the average rate of change from hour 12 to hour 24. Explain what this means in the context of the problem.

ALGEBRA 1 - NGLS
Test 4
Part IV

Answer one question in this part. The correct answer will receive 6 credits. Clearly indicate the necessary steps, including appropriate formula substitutions, diagrams, graphs, charts, etc. For all questions in this part, a correct numerical answer with no work shown will receive only 1 credit. All answers should be written in the spaces provided. [6]

35. Lydia wants to take art classes. She compares the cost at two art centers. Center A charges $25 per hour and a registration fee of $25. Center B charges $15 per hour and a registration fee of $75. Lydia plans to take x hours of classes.

Write an equation that models this situation, where A represents the total cost of Center A.

Write an equation that models this situation, where B represents the total cost of Center B.

If Lydia wants to take 10 hours of classes, use your equations to determine which center will cost *less*.

(continued on next page)

(Question 35 continued)

Graph your equations for Center *A* and Center *B* on the set of axes below.

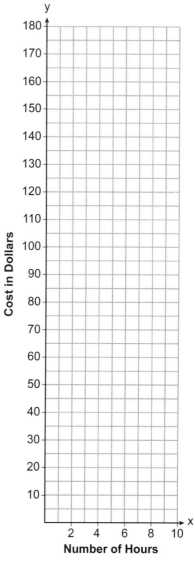

State the number of hours of classes when the centers will cost the same.

ALGEBRA 1
Next Generation Learning Standards
Test 5
Part I

Answer all 24 questions in this part. Each correct answer will receive 2 credits. No partial credit will be allowed. For each question, write on the space provided the numeral preceding the word or expression that best completes the statement or answers the question.

1. Ohm's Law of physics states that $V = IR$, where V is the voltage, I is the electric current, and R is the resistance. The formula is used to find measurements of voltage and current that travel through simple electrical circuits of differing lengths of wire. Which of the following states the law to highlight the current, I?
(1) $I = VR$ (2) $I = \dfrac{R}{V}$ (3) $R = \dfrac{V}{I}$ (4) $I = \dfrac{V}{R}$ 1 _____

2. The expression $64 - x^4$ is equivalent to which other expression?
(1) $(8 - x^2)(8 - x^2)$ (3) $(x^2 - 8)(x^2 - 8)$
(2) $(8 - x^2)(8 + x^2)$ (4) $(x^2 - 8)(x^2 + 8)$ 2 _____

3. The accompanying table represents Emilio's savings account for the last full year. Which function represents the account balance in terms of his monthly savings?

Month	Balance
1	62
2	74
3	86
4	98
5	110
6	122
7	134
8	146
9	158
10	170
11	182
12	194

(1) $f(x) = 12x + 50$
(2) $f(x) = 50x - 12$
(3) $f(x) = 12x - 50$
(4) $f(x) = 12x$

3 _____

4. Which equation is equivalent to $x^2 - 6x + 4 = 0$?
(1) $(x - 3)^2 = -4$ (3) $(x - 3)^2 = 6$
(2) $(x - 3)^2 = 5$ (4) $(x - 3)^2 = 9$ 4 _____

5. How many solutions are there for this linear quadratic system of equations? $y = x^2 + 2x - 3$; $y = 2x - 3$
(1) one (2) two (3) infinite (4) none   5 _____

6. The expression $-4.9t^2 + 50t + 2$ represents the height, in meters, of a toy rocket t seconds after launch. The initial height of the rocket, in meters, is
(1) 0 (2) 2 (3) 4.9 (4) 50   6 _____

ALGEBRA 1 - NGLS
Test 5

7. Which situation could be modeled with a linear function?
(1) the height of a ball that is thrown in the air
(2) the price of a car that depreciates 20% per year
(3) the amount of money Jonathan pays for a certain number of gallons of gas at $3.85 per gallon
(4) a bacteria colony which doubles in number every 4 hours   7 _____

8. A physics lab group was conducting an experiment to determine the length of a spring when different objects of varying weight were hung from it. After testing ten different objects, the group calculated the following linear regression where x is the weight of the object in ounces and $h(x)$ is the length of the spring in centimeters: $h(x) = 2.3x + 15.5$. What does y-intercept of this equation indicate about the relationship between object weight and the length of the spring?
(1) When there is no object on the spring, its length is 2.3 cm.
(2) When there is no object on the spring, its length 15.5 cm.
(3) For every ounce of weight, the spring length increases by 2.3 cm.
(4) For every ounce of weight, the spring length increases by 15.5 cm.   8 _____

9. The shaded boxes in the figures below represent a sequence.

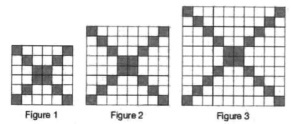

Figure 1   Figure 2   Figure 3

If figure 1 represents the first term and this pattern continues, how many shaded blocks will be in figure 35?
(1) 55   (3) 420
(2) 148   (4) 805   9 _____

10. Which ordered pair is the solution to the following system of equations? $2y - 2x = 8$
    $y = 2x - 6$
(1) (-2, 2)   (2) (2, -2)   (3) (10, 14)   (4) (4, 3)   10 _____

11. If $f(x) = x^2 - 5x$ and $g(x) = 2x - 3$, which expression represents the product of these two functions?
(1) $x^2 - 3x - 3$ (3) $9x^2 - 15x$
(2) $2x^3 - 13x^2 + 15x$ (4) $2x^3 - 15x$ 11 _____

12. The function G(m) represents the amount of gasoline consumed by a car traveling m miles. An appropriate domain for this function would be
(1) integers   (3) nonnegative integers
(2) rational numbers   (4) nonnegative rational numbers   12 _____

ALGEBRA 1 - NGLS
Test 5

13. Identify the slope in the equation: $x - \frac{1}{2} = 3x - x + y$

(1) –2 (2) –1 (3) $\frac{1}{2}$ (4) $-\frac{1}{2}$

13 _____

14. Joseph conducted a science experiment involving the growth of bacteria. He measured the number of bacteria hourly for 6 hours. The data is summarized in the accompanying table. What type of model would best fit the data?

Hour	Number of Bacteria
0	300
1	470
2	725
3	1150
4	1800
5	2750
6	4400

(1) Linear
(2) Exponential
(3) Quadratic
(4) Absolute Value

14 _____

15. Which expresses the area of the square in terms of x? $(x - 2)$

(1) $x^2 + 4x - 4$ (2) $x^2 - 4x + 4$ (3) $2x^2 + 4x + 4$ (4) $2x^2 - 4x + 4$

15 _____

16. Which is the equation of the line passing through the point (4, 0) and with a slope of $-\frac{1}{2}$?

(1) $y = 2x - \frac{1}{2}$
(2) $y = -\frac{1}{2}x + 2$
(3) $y = \frac{1}{2}x + 2$
(4) $y = 2x + 4$

16 _____

17. If $h(x) = \begin{cases} x^2, \text{if } x < 1 \\ 2, \text{if } -1 \leq x \leq 1 \\ x, \text{if } x > 1 \end{cases}$ find $h(-3)$.

(1) –3 (2) 2 (3) 3 (4) 9

17 _____

18. What is the range for an absolute value function?

(1) $0 \leq y < \infty$ (2) $\infty < y \leq 0$ (3) $x < 0$ (4) $-\infty < y < \infty$

18 _____

19. Which of the following equations is equivalent to $x^2 - 4x - 13 = 0$?

(1) $(x - 2)^2 = 13$
(2) $(x - 2)^2 = 17$
(3) $(x - 4)^2 = 13$
(4) $(x - 4)^2 = 17$

19 _____

20. Which expression represents the perimeter of the accompanying isosceles triangle?

(1) $6x^3 + x^2 + x + 16$
(2) $6x^2 + x + 16$
(3) $7x^3 + x^2 + 16$
(4) $x^3 + 7x^2 + x + 16$

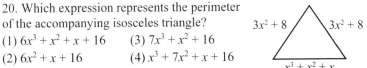

20 _____

ALGEBRA 1 - NGLS
Test 5

21. What is the difference when $(3x^2 - x - 2)$ is subtracted from $(6x^2 + 4x - 5)$?
(1) $3x^2 + 5x - 3$
(2) $3x^2 + 5x - 7$
(3) $9x^2 + 5x + 14$
(4) $9x^2 + 5x - 7$

21 _____

22. For which function is the value of the *y*-intercept the *smallest*?

x	f(x)
-4	5
-2	4
0	3
2	2
4	1

(1)

$g(x) = |x| + 4$

(2)

x	h(x)
-1	3
0	2
1	3
2	6
3	11

(3)

$k(x) = 5^x$

(4)

22 _____

23. Which histogram depicts data that is normally distributed?

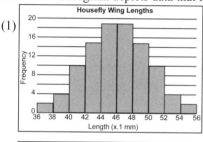
(1)

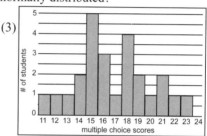
(3)

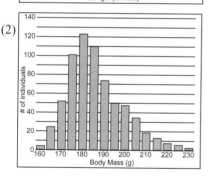
(2)

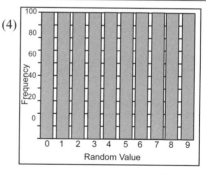
(4)

23 _____

24. The table below shows the number of reported polio cases in Nigeria from 2006 to 2015.

Year	2006	2007	2008	2009	2010	2011	2012	2013	2014	2015
Number of Cases	1129	285	798	388	21	62	122	53	60	0

What is the average rate of change, to the *nearest hundredth*, of the number of reported polio cases per year in Nigeria from 2006 to 2013?
(1) −0.01   (2) −125.44   (3) −134.50   (4) −153.71

24 _____

ALGEBRA 1 - NGLS
Test 5
Part II

Answer all 6 questions in this part. Each correct answer will receive 2 credits. Clearly indicate the necessary steps, including appropriate formula substitutions, diagrams, graphs, charts, etc. For all questions in this part, a correct numerical answer with no work shown will receive only 1 credit. All answers should be written in pen, except for graphs and drawings, which should be done in pencil. [16]

25. A small country in Europe has been experiencing population growth that can be modeled by the equation $y = 120,000(1.042)^x$ where y is the population of the country and x is the number of years since 2010. What is the percent change in the population of the country each year?

26. Joey can assemble all of his factory work in four hours. Phil takes six hours to assemble the same amount of factory work. If they worked together to assemble the same job together, how long would it take?

27. Solve by completing the square:
$$x^2 - 6x + 2 = 0$$

28. Renee has a jewelry business where her clients create their own bracelets from antique buttons. She charges $15 for the entire activity, which includes the string for the bracelet. It is an additional $2.00 for each antique button. Write an equation that represents the cost, given that x number of buttons are chosen.

29. Solve $x^2 + 3x - 9 = 0$ algebraically for all values of x. Round your answers to the *nearest hundredth*.

30. Solve: $\frac{1}{4}x = \frac{1}{20}x + 1$

ALGEBRA 1 - NGLS
Test 5
Part III

Answer all 4 questions in this part. Each correct answer will receive 4 credits. Clearly indicate the necessary steps, including appropriate formula substitutions, diagrams, graphs, charts, etc. For all questions in this part, a correct numerical answer with no work shown will receive only 1 credit. All answers should be written in pen, except for graphs and drawings, which should be done in pencil. [16]

31. A software company kept a record of their annual budget for advertising and their profit for each of the last eight years. These data are shown in the accompanying table.

Annual Advertising Budget (in thousands, $) (x)	Profit (in millions, $) (y)
10	2.2
13	2.4
14	3.2
16	4.6
19	5.7
24	6.9
24	7.9
28	9.3

Write the linear regression equation for this set of data.

State, to the *nearest hundredth*, the correlation coefficient of these linear data.

State what this correlation coefficient indicates about the linear fit of the data.

32. The graph of a first-degree absolute value function has a y-intercept of 3, x-intercepts of –9 and –3, and a minimum value of –3 at x = –6. On the axes provided, sketch a graph of this function.

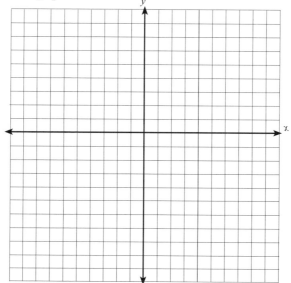

33. The senior class at Hills High School is purchasing sports drinks and bottled water to sell at the school field day. At the local discount store, a case of sports drinks costs $15.79, and a case of bottled water costs $5.69. The senior class has $125 to spend on the drinks.

If x represents the number of cases of sports drinks and y represents the number of cases of bottled water purchased, write an inequality that models this situation.

Nine cases of bottled water are purchased for this year's field day. Use your inequality to determine algebraically the maximum number of full cases of sports drinks that can be purchased.

Explain your answer.

ALGEBRA 1 - NGLS
Test 5

34. You are looking to join a monthly coffee delivery club. Your search has been narrowed down to the two top-rated clubs on the Internet. Five Star Coffee charges a $40 startup fee and then $8 per month. Custom Coffee Company charges a $25 startup fee and $12.50 per month. [The use of the grid below is optional.]

Write a linear function for each situation.

After how many months would both coffee clubs be the same value?

After one year, which coffee club would be the cheapest?

ALGEBRA 1
Next Generation Learning Standards
Part IV

Answer one question in this part. The correct answer will receive 6 credits. Clearly indicate the necessary steps, including appropriate formula substitutions, diagrams, graphs, charts, etc. For all questions in this part, a correct numerical answer with no work shown will receive only 1 credit. All answers should be written in pen, except for graphs and drawings, which should be done in pencil. [6]

35. Graph the following piecewise-defined function on the axes provided.

$$f(x) = \begin{cases} x + 2; \text{ if } x \leq 0 \\ x^2 - 2; \text{ if } x > 0 \end{cases}$$

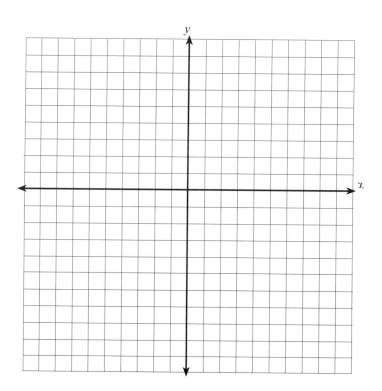

ALGEBRA 1
Next Generation Learning Standards
Test 6
Part I

Answer all 24 questions in this part. Each correct answer will receive 2 credits. No partial credit will be allowed. For each question, write on the space provided the numeral preceding the word or expression that best completes the statement or answers the question.

1. Which graph can represent a portion of a car race in which the driver makes two stops for fuel?

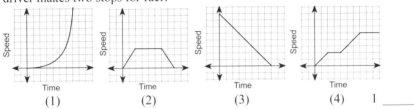

(1) (2) (3) (4)   1 _____

2. Which function has no x-intercept(s)?
(1) $y = 4x$ (2) $y = 4^x$ (3) $y = 4x^2$ (4) $y = 4 - x$ 2 _____

3. Which point is in the solution set to the quadratic linear system?
$$y = 2x^2 + x - 5 \text{ and } y + 3 = x$$
(1) $(1, -2)$ (2) $(1, 2)$ (3) $(-1, -2)$ (4) $(1, 2)$ 3 _____

4. Which function is equivalent to $f(x) = \begin{cases} -3x + 6; x < 2 \\ 3x - 6; x \geq 2 \end{cases}$?
(1) $f(x) = |-3x - 6|$ (3) $f(x) = |3x - 6|$
(2) $f(x) = -|3x + 6|$ (4) $f(x) = -|-3x - 6|$ 4 _____

5. The expression $9m^2 - 100$ is equivalent to
(1) $(3m - 10)(3m + 10)$ (3) $(3m - 50)(3m + 50)$
(2) $(3m - 10)(3m - 10)$ (4) $(3m - 50)(3m - 50)$ 5 _____

6. Which correlation coefficient indicates the strongest linear relationship between the variables?
(1) 0.79   (2) 0.52   (3) –0.63   (4) –0.84   6 _____

7. The tables below show the amount of money in different bank customer's accounts on the first day of each month for five months. Which customer's account increased at a constant rate per month?

(1)
Customer 1	
Months	Money
1	100
2	200
3	400
4	800
5	1600

(2)
Customer 2	
Months	Money
1	100
2	150
3	225
4	337.5
5	506.25

(3)
Customer 3	
Months	Money
1	100
2	200
3	300
4	200
5	100

(4)
Customer 4	
Months	Money
1	100
2	200
3	300
4	400
5	500

7 _____

ALGEBRA 1 - NGLS
Test 6

8. Jerome collects stamps. He saved up $100 to buy stamps to add to his collection. The stamps cost $1.50, $2, or $5. Which equation models the different ways that Jerome can spend his money where x represents the $1.50 stamps, y represents the $2 stamps, and z represents the $5 stamps?
(1) $7.50x = 100$
(2) $15xyz = 100$
(3) $1.5x + 2y + 5z = 100$
(4) $\frac{x}{1.5} + \frac{y}{2} + \frac{z}{5} = 100$

8 _____

9. Given $f(x)$ represented in the table and $g(x)$ represented in the graph, which is a true statement about the graphs in the interval $-5 < x < 0$?

x	y
-2	2
-1	3
0	4
1	5

(1) one function is increasing while the other function is decreasing
(2) both functions are increasing
(3) both functions are decreasing
(4) neither function is increasing

9 _____

10. In the equation $x^2 - 6x + 8 = 0$, what are the solutions for x?
(1) {4, 2} (2) {-4, 2} (3) {4, -2} (4) {-4, -2}

10 _____

11. Which is an example of bivariate data?
(1) age of students in a club
(2) grade level and age of students in a school
(3) type of lunch each student orders at school
(4) attendance numbers for all students in one grade

11 _____

12. The height of a rocket, at selected times, is shown in the table below.

Time (sec)	0	1	2	3	4	5	6	7
Height (ft)	180	260	308	324	308	260	180	68

Based on these data, which statement is not a valid conclusion?
(1) The rocket was launched from a height of 180 feet.
(2) The maximum height of the rocket occurred 3 seconds after launch.
(3) The rocket was in the air approximately 6 seconds before hitting the ground.
(4) The rocket was above 300 feet for approximately 2 seconds.

12 _____

13. The formula for the volume of a cone is $V = \frac{1}{3}\pi r^2 h$. Which is the correct equation that can be used for finding the height of the cone?
(1) $h = 3V(\pi r^2)$
(2) $h = \frac{3V}{\pi r^2}$
(3) $h = 3\pi r^2$
(4) $\frac{r^2}{3V}$

13 _____

14. Which quadratic graph opens upward?
(1) $y = 3x^2 - 4x - 1$
(2) $y = -3x^2 - 1$
(3) $y = -x^2$
(4) $y = -x^2 + 3x + 2$

14 _____

15. The function $f(x) = \sqrt{x}$. Which function represents a shift of the graph left 3 units?
(1) $f(x - 3) = \sqrt{x - 3}$
(2) $f(x + 3) = \sqrt{x + 3}$
(3) $f(x) + 3 = \sqrt{x} + 3$
(4) $f(x) - 3 = \sqrt{x} - 3$

15 ____

16. Which graph below shows a data set that is non-symmetric and skewed right?

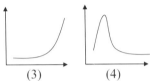

16 ____

17. Which statement is *not* always true?
(1) The product of two irrational numbers is irrational.
(2) The product of two rational numbers is rational.
(3) The sum of two rational numbers is rational.
(4) The sum of a rational number and an irrational number is irrational.

17 ____

18. Which relation is a function?
(1) {(0, 1), (0, 2), (0, 3), (0, 4)}
(2) {(3, 4), (4, 3), (5, 6), (6, 5)}
(3) {(1, 5), (2, 6), (3, 7), (3, 8)}
(4) {(1, 1), (4, 4), (1, 4), (4, 1)}

18 ____

19. What is the range for the following absolute value function, $y = |x|$?
(1) negative real numbers and zero
(2) positive real numbers and zero
(3) all real numbers
(4) zero

19 ____

20. Which of the following expressions can be written as the product of two binomial factors?
(1) $x^2 - 16$
(2) $x^2 + 16$
(3) $x^2 - 16x$
(4) $x^2 + 16x$

20 ____

21. Which sketch is the correct graph for the function $y = x^2 - 5x - 6$?

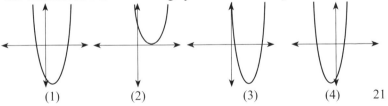

21 ____

22. John has four more nickels than dimes in his pocket, for a total of $1.25. Which equation could be used to determine the number of dimes, x, in his pocket?
(1) $0.10(x + 4) + 0.05(x) = \$1.25$
(2) $0.05(x + 4) + 0.10(x) = \$1.25$
(3) $0.10(4x) + 0.05(x) = \$1.25$
(4) $0.05(4x) + 0.10(x) = \$1.25$

22 ____

23. The graph represents the profit from a lemonade stand. The startup materials for the stand cost $3.00. How much is each cup of lemonade selling for?
(1) $0.10   (3) $0.50
(2) $0.25   (4) $1.00

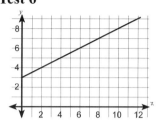

23 _____

24. Which function represents exponential decay?
(1) $f(x) = 100(.9)^x$ (3) $f(x) = 1.9^x$
(2) $f(x) = 10(1.09)^x$ (4) $f(x) = \frac{1}{2}(9)^x$

24 _____

Part II
Answer all 6 questions in this part. Each correct answer will receive 2 credits. Clearly indicate the necessary steps, including appropriate formula substitutions, diagrams, graphs, charts, etc. For all questions in this part, a correct numerical answer with no work shown will receive only 1 credit. All answers should be written in the space provided. [16]

25. Find the polynomial when $x^2 - 2x + 5$ is subtracted from $3x^2 + x + 1$.

26. Solve the inequality: $\dfrac{4(x+2)}{-4} \geq \dfrac{(x-7)}{2}$

27. If $g(x) = 3|x - 1|$ and $f(x) = |x|$, describe the transformation from $f(x)$ to $g(x)$.

28. Find the equation of the axis of symmetry of the graph: $y = -2x^2 + x - 1$

ALGEBRA 1 - NGLS
Test 6

29. Sasha wants to make the most money she can while maintaining a 90 average. Currently she makes $9.00 per hour at her job. She knows she can maintain a 100 average if she does not work at all. She has observed that for every two hours of work, her average goes down by one point. How much money can she make each week while still maintaining a 90 average?

30. Sam's profit after a year of selling custom bicycles that he has created can be represented by the function $f(x) = 325x - 1000$.

Complete the accompanying table that represents his profits from the past year.

In which month of the year did he begin to make a profit?

x	$f(x)$
3	
	625
7	
	2575

ALGEBRA 1 - NGLS
Test 6
Part III

Answer all 4 questions in this part. Each correct answer will receive 4 credits. Clearly indicate the necessary steps, including appropriate formula substitutions, diagrams, graphs, charts, etc. For all questions in this part, a correct numerical answer with no work shown will receive only 1 credit. All answers should be written in pen, except for graphs and drawings, which should be done in pencil. [16]

31. The path of a rocket is modeled by the function $h(t) = -4.9t^2 + 49t$, where h is the height, in meters, above the ground and t is the time, in seconds, after the rocket is launched.

Sketch the graph on the set of axes.

State the vertex of this function.

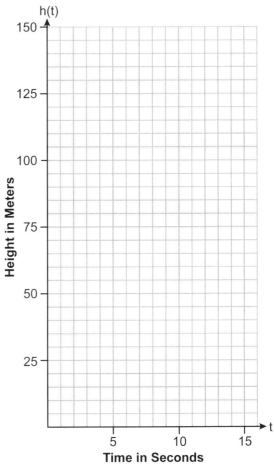

Explain what the vertex means in the context of this situation.

ALGEBRA 1 - NGLS
Test 6

32. Complete the two-way table below for the gender of students taking each course using conditional relative frequencies. The data is based on the senior English elective taken by students at Buchanan High School.

	Gender		Total
	Boys	Girls	
Creative Writing	65	150	
Visual Storytelling	70	120	
Newspaper Journalism	88	56	
Graphic Design	74	136	
Total			

What is the percent of girls enrolled in Visual Storytelling?
Round answer to the *nearest hundredth*. Justify your answer.

Of the students who take Graphic Design, what percentage are girls?
Round answer to the *nearest hundredth*. Justify your answer.

ALGEBRA 1 - NGLS
Test 6

33. g is a function that squares the input, x, and adds five to determine the output.

Write a function that models the relationship described.

Sketch the graph of $y = g(x)$ over the domain $-3 \leq x \leq 3$.

ALGEBRA 1 - NGLS
Test 6

34. Michelle found a bank account that offers 3.7% interest, compounded annually. She decides to put $100 in an account and leave it there for 10 years.

Write a function to model the growth of her investment t years after she put the money in the bank.

Sketch the graph of the function over the first ten years. Use an appropriate scale and label the axes.

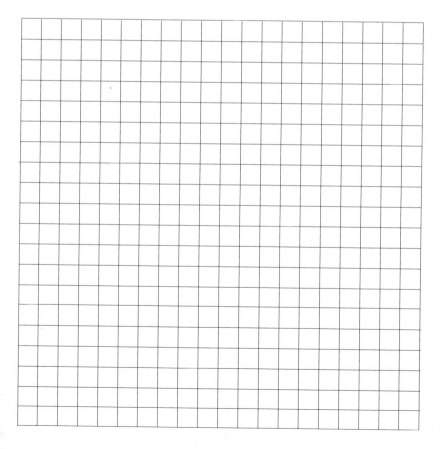

ALGEBRA 1 - NGLS
Test 6
Part IV

Answer one question in this part. The correct answer will receive 6 credits. Clearly indicate the necessary steps, including appropriate formula substitutions, diagrams, graphs, charts, etc. For all questions in this part, a correct numerical answer with no work shown will receive only 1 credit. All answers should be written in the spaces provided. [6]

35. Dana went shopping for plants to put in her garden. She bought three roses and two daisies for $31.88. Later that day, she went back and bought two roses and one daisy for $18.92.

If r represents the cost of one rose and d represents the cost of one daisy, write a system of equations that models this situation.

Use your system of equations to algebraically determine both the cost of one rose and the cost of one daisy.

If Dana had waited until the plants were on sale, she would have paid $4.50 for each rose and $6.50 for each daisy. Determine the total amount of money she would have saved by buying all of her flowers during the sale.